Twenty to Make

Knitted
Bears
All dressed up!

Val Pierce

Search Press

First published in Great Britain 2010

Search Press Limited
Wellwood, North Farm Road,
Tunbridge Wells, Kent TN2 3DR

Reprinted 2010 (three times), 2011 (twice),
2012 (twice), 2013

Text copyright © Val Pierce 2010
www.crossedneedles.co.uk

Photographs by Debbie Patterson at Search Press
Photographic Studio

Photographs and design copyright
© Search Press Ltd 2010

Print ISBN: 978-1-84448-482-9
Epub ISBN: 978-1-78126-018-0
Mobi ISBN: 978-1-78126-073-9
PDF ISBN: 978-1-78126-127-9

The Publishers and author can accept no
responsibility for any consequences arising from
the information, advice or instructions given in
this publication.

Readers are permitted to reproduce any of the
items in this book for their personal use, or for
the purposes of selling for charity, free of charge

Suppliers
If you have difficulty in obtaining any of the
materials and equipment mentioned in this book,
then please visit the Search Press website for
details of suppliers: www.searchpress.com

Printed in Malaysia

Dedication
To my late mum, Lorna, who taught me
all my crafting skills. Her inspiration will
always be with me.

Abbreviations
alt: alternate
rem: remaining
beg: beginning
cm: centimetres
sl: slip stitch
skpo: slip one, knit one, pass slipped
stitch over
dec: decrease
st(s): stitch(es)
tog: together
inc: increase
WS: wrong side
K: knit
RS: right side
P: purl
yfwd: yarn forward over needle to make
a hole
yrn: yarn around needle
psso: pass slipped stitch over
GS: garter stitch (knit every row)
SS: stocking stitch (one row knit, one
row purl)

UK and US terminology

UK	US
cast off	bind off
moss stitch	seed stitch
stocking stitch	stockinette stitch
yarn forward	yarn over

Needle conversion chart

Metric	US	Old UK
3.25mm	3	10
4.00mm	7	8

Contents

Introduction

Teddy bears have been a big favourite with both young and old for many, many years. In this book I have created a set of charming little characters for you to knit. Each one has its own special outfit, right down to its tiny shoes. The bears measure just 20cm (8in) tall and and are knitted in simple garter stitch, taking just a few hours to make. You will only need small amounts of yarn to knit both the bears and the variety of clothes I have designed. Use up all the leftover yarns in your stash, and either follow my colour choices or use your imagination and make up your own. Whatever you decide to do, I am sure that you will be thrilled with the outcome.

Happy knitting to you all, and remember:

Your teddy bear's a treasure,
a comfort to behold.
He'll love you when you're tiny,
as well as when you're old.
He's always there to listen,
to lend a furry ear.
No matter how you treat him,
He'll always hold you dear.
Don't throw him in the corner,
or leave him on the mat,
always take him with you,
he'll be very pleased with that!

Basic patterns

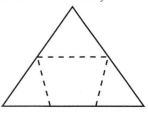

Bear:

Materials
1 ball double knitting yarn

Small quantity of soft textured, high quality safety stuffing

2 x 6mm round black beads for eyes

Black embroidery thread or floss for features

Sewing needles

Stitch holder

Needles
1 pair 3.25mm (UK 10; US 3) knitting needles

Instructions
Work entirely in GS, unless otherwise stated.

Head
Cast on 30 sts.
Rows 1–4: GS.
Row 5: K2, skpo, knit to last 3 sts, K2tog, K1.
Rows 6–7: GS.
Continue to dec in this way on every third row until 8 sts rem.
Next row: K2, skpo, K2tog, K2.
Next row: K2, skpo, K2.
Next row: K1, sl1, K2tog, psso, K1.
Next row: K3tog.
Fasten off.

Body and legs (make two pieces the same)
Cast on 12 sts.
Rows 1–2: GS.
Rows 3–8: inc 1 st at each end of rows 3, 5 and 7 [18 sts].
Rows 8–33: knit.
Row 34: divide for legs. K8, cast-off 2, knit to end [8 sts]. Proceed on these 8 sts for first leg.
Rows 35–52: knit.
Row 53: K2tog, knit to last 2 sts, K2tog.

Row 54: cast off.
Return to stitches left on needle, rejoin yarn and complete to match first leg.

Arms (make two)
Cast on 6 sts.
Row 1: knit.
Row 2: knit twice into each st to end [12 sts].
Rows 3–6: knit.
Row 7: inc 1 st at each end of row [14 sts].
Rows 8–27: knit.
Rows 28–30: dec 1 st at each end of rows 28 and 30 [10 sts].
Row 31: K2, (K2tog) 3 times, K2 [7 sts].
Row 32: knit.
Cast off (this is the top of the arm).

Making up
1. Make up the head by folding the three corners of the triangle into the centre; the fold lines are shown in the top diagram opposite. Sew the two side seams either side of the nose, and across the corner lines to form the ears, as shown in the lower diagram.
2. Sew a little way along the neck seam, just down from the nose. Stuff the head firmly to give it a good shape. Stitch on the nose and mouth with black thread, and sew on the eyes.
3. Stitch the back and front body pieces together using a flat seam on the right side of the work. Leave the neck edge open for stuffing. Stuff firmly and then close the neck opening. Seam the arms and stuff, then attach the head and arms to the body.

Shoes (make two):

Using an appropriate colour and 3.25mm (UK 10; US 3) needles, cast on 14 sts.
Next row: knit.
Next row: inc in each st across row [28 sts].
Work 5 rows GS.
Next row: K2tog, K8, (K2tog) 4 times, K8, K2tog.
Next row: K9, (K2tog) twice, K9.
Next row: knit.
Cast off. Stitch the seam along the base and back of the shoe. Put a tiny amount of stuffing inside the shoe, place the base of the leg inside the shoe and stitch it in place.
Add embellishments.

Trousers (make two pieces the same):

Using an appropriate colour and 3.25mm (UK 10; US 3) needles, cast on 13 sts.
Rows 1–4: GS.
Rows 5–20: SS, ending on a purl row. Break yarn and leave these 13 sts on a spare needle.
Now work another piece to match. Do not break off yarn but continue as follows:
Knit across 13 sts on needle, cast on 2 sts, work across 13 sts left on spare needle [28 sts].
Next row: purl.

*Work a further 2 rows in SS, ending on a purl row.
Next row: K2, skpo, knit to last 4 sts, K2tog, K2.
Next row: purl.*
Repeat from * to * [24 sts].
Work 4 rows in rib, or as given in instructions.

Dress:

Bodice front

Cast on 24 sts.
Rows 1–6: SS.
Rows 7–8: cast off 2 sts at beg of each row.
Rows 9–10: SS.
Row 11: dec 1 st at each end of row [18 sts].
Row 12: purl.
Rows 13–16: SS.

Divide for neck

Work 7 sts, slip next 4 sts on to stitch holder for neck, turn and work 7 sts.
Continue on first 7 sts for side of neck.
Dec 1 st at neck edge on next and following alt rows until 4 sts rem.
Cast off.
Work other side to match.

Bodice back

Work rows 1–16 of bodice front.
Rows 17–21: SS.
Cast off.

Skirt

With RS facing, pick up and knit 24 sts along cast-on edge of bodice front.
Next row: purl.
Next row: knit twice into each st [48 sts].
Continue in SS and complete as given in pattern.
Repeat the above, on bodice back.

Neckband

Join one shoulder seam.
With RS facing, pick up and

knit 5 sts down one side of neck, 4 sts from stitch holder across front of neck, 5 sts up other side of neck and 10 sts around back of neck (rem 4 sts will form other shoulder).
Next row: knit.
Cast off knitwise.

Katy Strawberry Bear

Materials:

1 ball strawberry pink double knitting

1 ball pale green double knitting

Small amount of safety stuffing

1 large and 2 small flower buttons

Small gold beads for seeds on strawberry

Materials for basic bear, including light beige
    double knitting

Needles:

1 pair 3.25mm (UK 10; US 3) knitting needles

Instructions:

Make the basic bear (see page 6).

Strawberry body

The two body parts are worked in strawberry
pink yarn. Make two pieces the same, each
beginning at the base, working in SS.

Cast on 8 sts, and work rows 1–2 SS.
Rows 3–7: continuing in SS, inc 1 st at each end
of rows 3, 5 and 7 [14 sts].
Row 8: purl.
Rows 9–10: cast on 2 sts at beg of each row.
Rows 11–12: cast on 3 sts at beg of each row
[24 sts].
Rows 13–15: inc 1 st at each end of rows 13 and
15 [28 sts].
Rows 16–21: SS, beg with a purl row.
Rows 22–28: dec 1 st at each end of rows 22, 24,
26 and 28 [20 sts].
Rows 29–30: SS, ending with a purl row.
Rows 31–32: cast off 2 sts at beg of each row.
Row 33: dec 1 st at each end of row.
Rows 34–36: SS.
Cast off.

Collar leaves (make five)

Work all inc sts for the collar leaves by picking
up the strand of yarn between the previous 2
sts and knitting into the back of it.
Using pale green, cast on 5 sts.
Row 1: purl.
Row 2: K2, inc, K1, inc, K2 [7 sts].
Row 3: knit.

Row 4: K3, inc, K1, inc, K3 [9 sts].
Row 5: knit.
Row 6: K4, inc, K1, inc, K4 [11 sts].
Row 7: knit.
Row 8: K5, inc, K1, inc, K5 [13 sts].
Rows 9–13: knit.
Row 14: K2tog, knit to last 2 sts, K2tog [11 sts].
Row 15: knit.
Row 16: repeat row 14 [9 sts].
Row 17: knit.
Row 18: repeat row 14 [7 sts].
Row 19: K2tog, K3, K2tog [5 sts].
Row 20: K2tog, K1, K2tog [3 sts].
Row 21: P3tog. Fasten off.

Small leaf

Using pale green, cast on 3 sts.
Next row: K1, inc in next st, K1 [4 sts].
Work 4 rows GS.
Next row: dec 1 st at each end of row.
Next row: K2tog.
Fasten off.

Shoes

Follow basic shoes pattern (page 7), using
pale green.

Making up

Stitch the body parts together at the base and
sew up the side seams. Slip the body on to
the bear and place small amounts of stuffing
into the space between the bear and the body,
shaping it as you go. Stitch the shoulder seams.
Catch the body in places around the legs and

the armholes, and along the neck edge. Sew on gold beads randomly to represent seeds. Sew the shoes on to the bear and stitch the small flower buttons on to the shoe fronts. Sew the large flower button and small leaf on to the bear's head. Sew the five larger leaves together in a circle to form the collar, and stitch in place around the bear's neck.

Oliver Baby Bear

Materials:
1 ball white double knitting

1 ball blue double knitting

50cm (19¾in) narrow, pale blue ribbon

1 comforter button

Tiny iron-on teddy nursery motif

Materials for basic bear, including light brown double knitting

Needles:
1 pair 3.25mm (UK 10; US 3) knitting needles

Instructions:
Make the basic bear (see page 6). When making up the bear, sew across the tops of the legs where they join to the body, so that the legs bend.

Top (make two pieces, front and back)
Using blue yarn, cast on 24 sts.

Row 1: knit.

Work in pattern as follows:

Row 2: (WS facing) (K1, P1) to end of row.

Row 3: knit.

Rows 4–7: repeat rows 2 and 3, twice.

Rows 8–9: continuing in pattern, cast off 2 sts at beg of each row.

Rows 10–19: repeat rows 2 and 3, 5 times.

Rows 20–23: GS.

Cast off.

Nappy
Using white yarn, cast on 24 sts.

Rows 1–4: work in K1, P1 rib.

Rows 5–10: SS.

Continue in SS.

To shape legs:

Rows 11–12: cast off 4 sts at beg of each row.

Rows 13–14: cast off 3 sts at beg of each row.

Row 15: K2tog at each end of row [8 sts].

Row 16: purl.

Rows 17–18: repeat rows 15 and 16 [6 sts].

Rows 19–28: SS.

Rows 29–31: inc 1 st at each end of rows 29 and 31 [10 sts].

Row 32: purl.

Rows 33–34: cast on 3 sts at beg of each row.

Rows 35–36: cast on 4 sts at beg of each row [24 sts].

Rows 37–42: SS.

Rows 43–46: (K1, P1) rib to end of row.

Cast off in rib.

Bootees
Using blue yarn, follow instructions for basic shoes on page 7.

Making up
Work in the ends, sew the side seams of the nappy and slip the nappy on to the bear. Sew the side seams of the bear's top, slip it on to the bear and catch the shoulder seams together. Iron the motif on to the front of the top. Tie the comforter button on to a length of ribbon and hang it around the bear's neck. Sew up the seams of the bootees, tie tiny bows and attach them to the fronts. Sew the bootees on to the bear.

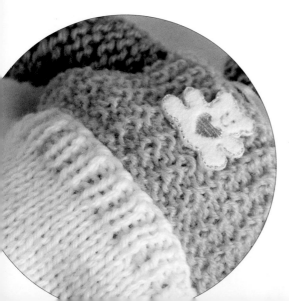

Peter Pumpkin Bear

Materials:

1 ball green double knitting

1 ball orange double knitting

Oddments of brown double knitting

Black felt for pumpkin features

Small amount of safety stuffing

Materials for basic bear, including green
  double knitting

Needles:

1 pair 3.25mm (UK 10; US 3) knitting needles

Instructions:

Make the basic bear (see page 6).

Pumpkin body

Make two body pieces the same, starting at the
base. Work in SS.

Using orange, cast on 8 sts and work rows 1
and 2 in SS.

Rows 3–7: continuing in SS, inc 1 st at each end
of rows 3, 5 and 7 [14 sts].

Row 8: purl.

Rows 9–10: cast on 2 sts at beg of each row.

Rows 11–12: cast on 3 sts at beg of each row
[24 sts].

Rows 13–15: inc 1 st at each end of rows 13 and
15 [28 sts].

Rows 16–21: SS, beg with a purl row.

Rows 22–30: dec 1 st at each end of rows 22, 24,
26 and 30 [20 sts].

Rows 31–32: SS, ending with a purl row.

Rows 33–34: cast off 2 sts at beg of each row.

Row 35: dec 1 st at each end of row [14 sts].

Rows 36–38: SS (this is the neck edge).

Cast off.

Hat

Using orange, cast on 8 sts.

Row 1: purl.

Row 2: inc in each st to end of row [16 sts].

Row 3: purl.

Row 4: (K1, inc in next st) to end.

Row 5: purl.

Row 6: (K2, inc in next st) to end.

Rows 7–9: SS, beg with a purl row.

Cast off.

Pumpkin stalk

Using brown, cast on 6 sts.

Rows 1–5: GS.

Cast off.

Leaves (make two)

Work all inc sts for the leaves by picking up the
strand of yarn between the previous 2 sts and
knitting into the back of it.

Using green, cast on 5 sts.

Row 1: purl.

Row 2: K2, inc, K1, inc, K2 [7 sts].

Row 3: knit.

Row 4: K3, inc, K1, inc, K3 [9 sts].

Rows 5–8: knit.

Dec 1 st at each end of every following alt row
until 3 sts rem.

K3tog.

Fasten off.

Making up

Stitch the body parts together at the base,
then join the side seams. Slip the body on to
the bear and stuff lightly to give a rounded

shape. Sew the shoulder seams, then secure the body to the bear by stitching all around the armholes and legs. Sew up the hat seam, stitch the stalk together lengthwise, and attach the stalk to the top of the hat. Stuff the hat lightly and sew it to the head. Cut out shapes for the eyes, nose and mouth from black felt (use the photograph as a guide). Stitch them in place. Stitch the leaves together and secure to the bear's shoulder.

Freddy Football Bear

Materials:

1 ball white double knitting

1 ball red double knitting

Oddment of black double knitting for boots and embroidery

Small amount of safety stuffing

Materials for basic bear, including yellow double knitting

Needles:

1 pair 3.25mm (UK 10; US 3) knitting needles

Instructions:

Make the basic bear (see page 6). When working the legs, after 4 rows of yellow change to the stripe pattern of 2 rows red, 2 rows white for the socks.

Shirt
Back:
Using red, cast on 24 sts.
Rows 1–4: K2, P2 rib.
Rows 5–10: change to white and SS for 6 rows, beg with a knit row.
To shape armholes (raglan shaping):
Rows 11–12: cast off 2 sts at beg of each row.
Row 13: K1, skpo, knit to last 3 sts, K2tog, K1.
Row 14: purl.
Repeat rows 13–14 until 8 sts rem, ending on a purl row. Leave sts on a stitch holder.

Sleeves (make two):
Using red, cast on 24 sts.
Rows 1–4: K2, P2 rib.
Rows 5–8: change to white and SS for 4 rows.
Shape top as for back.

Front:
Work as back until 14 sts rem after raglan shaping, then divide for neck.
Next row: K1, skpo, K2, turn and leave rem sts on a stitch holder.
Next row: purl.
Next row: K1, skpo, K1.
Next row: purl.
Next row: K3tog.
Fasten off.

Slip first 4 sts on to safety pin for centre neck, join yarn to remaining sts and complete to match first side, reversing shaping and working K2tog in place of skpo.

Neckband:
Using red, pick up and knit 8 sts across top of sleeve, then 5 sts down left side of neck, 4 sts across centre front, 5 sts up right side of neck, 8 sts across other sleeve and 8 sts across back.
GS for 3 rows.
Cast off firmly.

Shorts (make two pieces the same)
Using white, cast on 13 sts.
Rows 1–2: GS.
Rows 3–8: SS, beg with a knit row.
Break yarn and leave these 13 sts on a spare needle.
Work another piece to match, but this time do not break off yarn. Continue as follows:
Row 9: knit across 13 sts on needle, cast on 2 sts, work across 13 sts left on spare needle [28 sts].
Row 10: purl.
Rows 11–12: SS, beg with a knit row.
Row 13: K1, skpo, knit to last 3 sts, K2tog, K1.
Row 14: purl.
Rows 15–18: repeat rows 11–14 [24 sts].
Rows 19–22: K2, P2 rib.
Cast off in rib.

Boots

Using black yarn, follow instructions for basic shoes on page 7. Once attached to the bear's legs, sew a few stitches using white yarn to represent laces.

Football

Using white yarn, make a ball following the instructions on pages 16–17.

Making up

Sew the seams on the shorts and put them on to the bear. Sew the seams on the shirt, but leave the back raglan seam and neckband open. Slip the shirt on to the bear and join up the remaining seam. Using black, embroider a number on the back using chain stitch and a tiny badge on the front; use the photograph as a guide.

Toby Toddler Bear

Materials

1 ball denim blue double knitting

Oddments of turquoise, green and orange yarn

Black embroidery thread

Small candy cane button

Small amount of safety stuffing

Materials for basic bear, including beige
  double knitting

Needles:

1 pair 3.25mm (UK 10; US 3) knitting needles

Instructions:

Make the basic bear (see page 6).

Dungarees

Front:
Using denim blue, cast on 13 sts.
Rows 1–4: GS.
Rows 5–20: SS, ending on a purl row. Break yarn
and leave these 13 sts on a spare needle.
Now work another piece to match. Do not
break off yarn but continue as follows:
Row 21: knit across 13 sts on needle, cast on 2
sts, work across 13 sts left on spare needle
[28 sts].
Row 22: purl.
Rows 23–24: SS, ending on a purl row.
Row 25: K2, skpo, knit to last 4 sts, K2tog, K2.
Row 26: purl.
Rows 27–30: repeat rows 23–26 [24 sts].
Rows 31–34: GS.

Bib:
Row 35: (RS facing) cast off 8 sts (1 st left on
needle), knit a further 7 sts, cast off rem 8 sts.
Turn and continue to work on rem 8 sts.
Row 36: (WS facing) K2, P4, K2.
Row 37: knit.
Rows 38–41: repeat rows 36–37 twice.
Row 42: as row 36.
Rows 43–46: GS.
Row 47: K2, cast off 4 sts, K2.
Working on first set of 2 sts for straps, continue
in GS until strap fits over shoulder and down to
waist on back of bear. Cast off.

Return to other set of 2 sts and make a second
strap to match. Cast off.

Back:
Work as front of dungarees (rows 1–34).
Cast off.

Patch:
Using a colour of your choice, cast on 6 sts.
Work 10 rows in GS.
Cast off.

Ball

Using turquoise, cast on 6 sts.
Row 1: purl.
Row 2: inc in each st across row [12 sts].
Row 3: purl.
Row 4: (K1, inc in next st) across row [18 sts].
Row 5: purl.
Row 6: (K2, inc in next st) across row [24 sts].
Row 7: purl.
Rows 8–9: SS.
Break yarn.
Change to orange yarn.
Rows 10–13: GS, beg with a knit row.
Break yarn and join in green yarn.
Rows 14–15: SS, ending with purl row.
Row 16: (K2, K2tog) across row [18 sts].
Row 17: purl.
Row 18: (K1, K2tog) across row [12 sts].
Row 19: purl.
Row 20: K2tog across row [6 sts].
Row 21: purl.
Break yarn and run end through rem sts. Pull up
tight and secure.

Making up

Sew the seams of the dungarees, slip them on to the bear, cross the straps behind the bear's head and secure them on the back waistband. Place the patch on the dungaree knee (as shown in the photograph) and stitch it in place using large stitches. For the ball, Sew the side seam, and stuff the ball to give a rounded shape before closing. Sew the candy cane button inside the waistband.

Billy Bridegroom Bear

Materials:

1 ball black double knitting

1 ball grey double knitting

Oddment of sparkly white double knitting for cravat

2 small gold beads for buttons

1 small, white paper rose

1 pearl bead

Materials for basic bear, including beige double knitting

Needles:

1 pair 3.25mm (UK 10; US 3) knitting needles

Instructions:

Make the basic bear (see page 6).

Waistcoat

Front (make two pieces the same and work in moss stitch):

Using grey, cast on 3 sts.

Row 1: K1, P1, K1.

Row 2: inc in next st, P1, inc in next st.

Row 3: P1, K1, P1, K1, P1.

Row 4: inc in next st, K1, P1, K1, inc in next st.

Row 5: (K1, P1) 3 times, K1.

Row 6: (K1, P1) 3 times, K1.

Row 7: (K1, P1) 3 times, K1.

Row 8: inc, (P1, K1) 2 times, P1, inc.

Row 9: (P1, K1) 4 times, P1.

Row 10: (P1, K1) 4 times, P1.

Row 11: inc, (K1, P1) 3 times, K1, inc.

Row 12: K1, P1, 5 times, K1.

Row 13: inc, (P1, K1) 4 times, P1, inc.

Row 14: (P1, K1) 6 times, P1 [13 sts].

Rows 15–16: continue in pattern.

Row 17: K2tog, pattern to end.

Row 18: cast off 2 sts, pattern to end.

Row 19: P2tog, pattern to last 2 sts, K2tog [8 sts].

Rows 20–26: dec 1 st at beg of row and at this edge on every alt row until 4 sts rem.

Rows 27–28: work in pattern.

Cast off.

Back:

Cast on 24 sts.

Rows 1–2: knit.

Rows 3–8: SS.

Shape arms and complete as for basic dress – bodice back (page 7).

Trousers

Using black yarn, follow instructions for basic trousers (page 7).

Cravat

Using white, cast on 16 sts.

Rows 1–20: SS, ending with a purl row.

Row 21: dec 1 st at each end of row.

Row 22: purl.

Repeat rows 21–22 until 10 sts remain.

Work 6 rows SS. Cast off.

Making up

Sew the shoulder seams of the waistcoat, then sew the side seams. Sew the wide edge of the cravat to the centre neck of the bear under his chin. Pouch it slightly then stitch the pearl bead on to the cravat to represent a tie pin. Put on the waistcoat and secure it with the two gold beads. Refer to the photograph as a guide. Sew the trouser seams and put the trousers on to the bear. Tuck the end of the cravat into the top of the trousers. Secure the white paper rose as a buttonhole in the waistcoat.

Grace Bride Bear

Materials:

1 ball sparkly white double knitting

Small piece of net for veil

Short length of narrow satin ribbon, pearl and rose embellishment for headdress

25cm (9¾in) narrow lace edging

6 white paper roses for bouquet

30 small pearl beads for necklace

Strong thread for sewing and for threading beads

1m (39½in) white satin ribbon, 5mm (¼in) wide

Materials for basic bear, including pale beige double knitting

Needles:

1 pair 3.25mm (UK 10; US 3) knitting needles

Instructions:

Make the basic bear (see page 6).

Dress

Using sparkly white yarn, follow instructions for basic dress on page 7, but when working the skirt continue until work measures 7cm (2¾in). Work 4 rows in moss stitch.
Cast off.

Making up the dress

Stitch one shoulder seam and work the neckband in moss stitch (see page 7). Sew the side seams, turn right-side out and slip the dress on to the bear. Catch together the neckband and the shoulder seam neatly. Tie the ribbon around the bear's waist and finish with a bow at the back.

Headdress and veil

Gather a short length of narrow satin ribbon into a circle, a little bigger than the pearl and rose embellishment, and secure it to the roses with a few stitches. Fold the net into an oblong and gather it at the top to give it a nice shape. Stitch it to the headdress.

Bouquet

Gather the lace edging into a circle. Slip the bunch of roses through the centre and secure. Sew each side of the bouquet to the bear's paws to hold it in place.

Necklace

Thread the pearl beads on to a piece of strong thread and make a string of them long enough to go around the bear's neck. Knot and secure. Tie the necklace around the bear's neck.

Pippa Dolly Bear

Materials:

1 ball deep mauve double knitting

1 ball lilac double knitting

25cm (9¾in) narrow ribbon in deep mauve

Tiny doll

2 small buttons

Tiny mauve bow embellishment

Materials for basic bear, including white
double knitting

Needles:

1 pair 3.25mm (UK 10; US 3) knitting needles

Instructions:

Make the basic bear (see page 6).

Dress
Back:
Using deep mauve, cast on 44 sts.
Rows 1–3: GS.
Change to lilac.
Rows 1–4 form the pattern.
Row 1: (RS) knit.
Row 2: purl.
Row 3: K2, *yrn, P1, P3tog, P1, yon, K2*, rep
from * to * to end.
Row 4: purl.
Rows 5–16: repeat rows 1–4, 3 times.
Row 17: K2tog across row [22 sts].
Row 18: knit.
Row 19: K2, (yfwd, K2tog, K1) to last 2 sts, yfwd,
K2tog.
Row 20: knit.
Rows 21–24: SS.
Row 25: cast off 2 sts, knit to end.
Row 26: cast off 2 sts, purl to end.
Row 27: K1, skpo, knit to last 3 sts, K2tog, K1.
Row 28: purl.
Repeat rows 27 and 28 until 6 sts rem, ending
on a purl row. Slip sts on to a stitch holder.

Sleeves (make two the same):
Using deep mauve, cast on 22 sts.
Rows 1–3: GS.
Change to lilac.

Rows 4–8: SS, ending with a purl row.
Continue from row 25 of the Dress Back,
ending with 6 sts. Slip sts on to a stitch holder.

Front:
Follow instructions for back to row 28.
Continue shaping until 12 sts remain, ending
with a purl row.

To shape neck:
Next row: K2, K2tog, turn. Leave rem sts on a
stitch holder.
Next row: purl.
Next row: K1, K2tog, turn.
Next row: purl.
Next row: K2tog, fasten off.
Return to sts on holder. Slip next 4 sts on to a
safety pin for front of neck.
Shape other side of neck:
Next row: K2tog, K2.
Next row: purl.
Next row: K2tog, K1.
Next row: purl.
Next row: K2tog.
Fasten off.

Neckband:
Using deep mauve, pick up and knit 31 sts all
around neck.
Work 3 rows GS.
Cast off.

Shoes

Using deep mauve yarn, follow instructions for basic shoes on page 7.

Making up

Sew the seams of the dress, but leave the left back raglan and neckband open. Slip the dress on to the bear and join the remaining seams.

Thread the ribbon through the holes at the waist and tie in a bow. Sew the shoes on to the bear (see page 7) and attach the button on the fronts. Attach the doll to the bear's paw with a few stitches and sew the paw to the body to hold it in place. Sew the tiny bow to the bear's head.

Holly Christmas Bear

Materials:

1 ball red double knitting

1 ball sparkly white double knitting

3 gold star buttons

1 candle button

1m (39½in) red satin ribbon, 5mm (¼in) wide

Materials for basic bear, including light beige double knitting

Needles:

1 pair 3.25mm (UK 10; US 3) knitting needles

Instructions:

Make the basic bear (see page 6).

Dress

Follow instructions for basic dress (see page 7), using red yarn.

When skirt measures 6cm (2¼in), change to white.

Work 3 rows GS.

Cast off.

Work the neckband using white.

Sleeves (make two the same):

Using white, cast on 24 sts.

Rows 1–2: knit.

Break yarn and join in red.

Rows 3–10: SS.

Cast off.

Boots

Using red yarn, follow instructions for basic shoes on page 7.

For tops of boots, cast on 16 sts in white and knit 2 rows. Cast off.

Muff

Using white, cast on 18 sts.

Rows 1–2: GS.

Join in red yarn.

Rows 3–12: SS, ending with a purl row.

Rows 13–14: GS, using white yarn.

Cast off.

Hat

Using white, cast on 36 sts.

Rows 1–10: GS.

Break white yarn and join in red.

Rows 11–16: SS.

To shape top of hat:

Row 17: (K4, skpo) across row [30 sts].

Rows 18–20: SS.

Row 21: (K3, skpo) across row [24 sts].

Row 22: purl.

Row 23: (K2, skpo) across row [18 sts].

Row 24: purl.

Row 25: K2tog across row [9 sts].

Break yarn and thread through rem sts. Pull tight and fasten off.

Making up

Sew the side seams of the dress and turn right-side out. Slip the dress on to the bear. Catch together the neckband and shoulder seam neatly. Sew the sleeve seams then stitch the sleeves to the armholes. Attach the boots to the bear's legs (see page 7). Stitch the white tops around the tops of the boots, attaching each one to the boot and to the bear's leg. Sew on the star buttons. Stitch the side seam of the muff, roll it into a cylinder shape and attach the star button to the front. Cut a length of ribbon long enough to form a strap and stitch it inside

the muff, making sure the ribbon join is hidden inside. Join the side seam of the hat and turn back the brim. Make a tiny pom-pom and sew it to the top of the hat. Place the hat on the bear's head and secure. Sew the candle button on the front.

Abi Ballet Bear

Materials:

1 ball pale pink double knitting

Pink net for under skirt, 10 x 40cm (4 x 15¾in)

1 pink satin ribbon, pearl and
   rose embellishment

4 small ribbon roses

50cm (19¾in) sparkly pink ribbon edging

Strong thread for sewing

1m (39½in) pink double-sided satin ribbon,
   5mm (¼in) wide

Materials for basic bear, including light beige
   double knitting

Needles:

1 pair 3.25mm (UK 10; US 3) knitting needles

Instructions:

Make the basic bear (see page 6).

Dress
Using pink yarn, follow instructions for basic
dress (see page 7).
When skirt measures 5cm (2in), work 2 rows GS.
Cast off.

Making up the dress:
Stitch one shoulder seam and work the
neckband. Sew the side seams, turn right-side
out and slip the dress on to the bear. Catch
together the neckband and shoulder seam. Tie

a length of ribbon around the waist and tie in a
bow at the back. Attach the ribbon, pearl and
rose embellishment to the front of the dress at
the waistline. Stitch the pink edging around the
hem and neckline.

Ballet slippers
Using pink yarn, follow instructions for basic
shoes on page 7, but work in SS. Attach the
slippers to the bear's legs following the basic
instructions. Take a short length of pink ribbon,
approximately 8cm (3¼in) long, and stitch one
end to the right-hand side of the left-hand
slipper at the front. Take it across the front of
the shoe to the left, and wrap it around the
back of the bear's leg. Bring it back round to
the front and catch it in place on the left-hand
side of the slipper. Sew a ribbon rose to the
centre front. Finish the other slipper to match.

Finishing off
Take the net and fold it in half lengthwise.
Gather the folded edge (this is the top) until
it fits around the bear's waist. Slip it on to the
bear and secure. Sew the side seam. Catch it in
place under the skirt of the dress. Make a small
bow with pink ribbon and stitch two ribbon
roses to the centre of it. Place the decoration
on the bear's head and stitch it in place. Use
the photograph as a guide.

Barney College Bear

Materials:

1 ball cream double knitting

1 ball deep turquoise double knitting

Materials for basic bear, including grey double knitting

Needles:

1 pair 3.25mm (UK 10; US 3) knitting needles

Instructions:

Make the basic bear (see page 6).

Sweatshirt

Front:

Using cream, cast on 26 sts.

Rows 1–3: moss stitch.

Rows 4–5: SS.

Now place the motif, using the chart for guidance:

Row 6: K10, join in turquoise and K7, change back to cream and K9. This forms the base of the 'B'.

Rows 7–15: continue working from the chart until the motif is complete.

Rows 16–18: SS.

Rows 19–21: moss stitch.

Cast off.

Back:

Work as front, but omit the motif.

Sleeves (make two the same):

Using cream, cast on 25 sts.

Rows 1–3: moss stitch.

Rows 4–5: SS.

Rows 6–7: join in turquoise, and SS.

Rows 8–9: SS using cream.

Rows 10–11: SS using turquoise.

Rows 12–13: SS using cream.

Cast off. (This is the top of the sleeve.)

Pants

Using turquoise yarn, follow instructions for basic trousers (page 7).

Side stripe:

Using cream, cast on 20 sts.

Knit 1 row.

Cast off.

Making up

Work in the yarn ends on the sweatshirt, and stitch the shoulder seams for 5 sts in from each side. Fold the sleeves in half lengthways and mark the centre point at the top. Stitch them in place along the sides of the sweatshirt, matching the centre point to the shoulder seam. Now join the side and sleeve seams. Slip the sweatshirt over the bear's head. Join the trouser seams, stitch the stripe on to the side seam and put the trousers on to the bear.

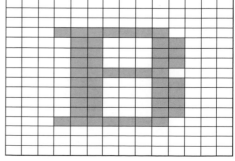

Sweet Honey Bee Bear

Materials:

1 ball black double knitting

1 ball yellow double knitting

1 ball cream double knitting

Small amount of safety stuffing

2 small silk flowers and a leaf

Materials for basic bear, including yellow and black double knitting

Needles:

1 pair 3.25mm (UK 10; US 3) knitting needles

Instructions:

Make the basic bear (see page 6) using black for the body, legs and arms and yellow for the head.

Bee body

The two body parts are worked in black and yellow yarn. Make two pieces the same, each beginning at the base, working in SS. Start with 6 rows yellow, then 4 rows black. Repeat

until the third black stripe is completed, then continue in yellow only.

Using yellow, cast on 8 sts.
Rows 1–2: SS.
Rows 3–7: continuing in SS, inc 1 st at each end of rows 3, 5 and 7 [14 sts].
Row 8: purl.
Rows 9–10: cast on 2 sts at beg of each row.
Rows 11–12: cast on 3 sts at beg of each row [24 sts].
Rows 13–15: inc 1 st at each end of rows 13 and 15 [28 sts].
Rows 16–21: SS, beg with a purl row.
Rows 22–28: dec 1 st at each end of rows 22, 24, 26 and 28 [20 sts].
Rows 29–30: SS, ending with a purl row.
Rows 31–32: cast off 2 sts at beg of each row.
Row 33: dec 1 st at each end of row [14 sts].
Rows 34–36: SS.
Cast off.

Wings

Large (make two):
Using cream, cast on 8 sts.
Rows 1–2: knit.
Rows 3–9: inc 1 st at each end of rows 3, 5, 7 and 9 [16 sts].
Rows 10–17: GS.
Rows 18–28: dec 1 st at each end of rows 18, 20, 22, 24, 26 and 28 [4 sts].
Cast off.

Small (make two):
Using cream, cast on 6 sts.
Rows 1–2: knit.
Rows 3–9: inc 1 st at each end of rows 3, 5, 7 and 9 [14 sts].
Rows 10–15: GS.
Dec 1 st at each end of next and every alt row until 4 sts remain.
Cast off.

Making up

Sew the base and side seams of the body pieces, matching the stripes. Slip the body on to the bear, stuff lightly to give a rounded shape, and sew the shoulder seams. Now catch the body pieces to the bear around the legs, arms and neck edge to secure. Sew the wings together in pairs, with the small wing on top of the large wing, and secure them to the bear at the back of the neck. Make the antennae using a piece of black yarn. Thread it through the top of the head. Roll each end into a tight circle and stitch to secure. Thread the flower stems through the paw and secure the paw to the body.

Olivia Sweetheart Bear

Materials:

1 ball cream double knitting

1 ball pink double knitting

Small piece of narrow pink ribbon

Materials for basic bear, including pale pink
double knitting

Needles:

1 pair 3.25mm (UK 10; US 3) knitting needles

Instructions:

Make the basic bear (see page 6).

Trousers

Follow instructions for basic trousers (see page
7). Work the first 4 rows of the trouser legs in
moss stitch using pink, and the remainder of
the trousers in SS stripes of 2 rows cream and
2 rows pink. The waistband is worked in
moss stitch.

Sweater

Back:
Using cream, cast on 25 sts.
Rows 1–4: moss stitch.
Rows: 5–10: SS.

To shape armholes:
Rows 11–12: continue in SS, and cast off 2 sts at
beg of each row.
Row 13: K1, skpo, knit to last 3 sts, K2tog, K1.
Row 14: purl.
Repeat rows 13 and 14 until 9 sts remain,
ending with a purl row. Leave sts on a
stitch holder.

Sleeves (make two the same):
Using cream, cast on 25 sts.
Rows 1–4: moss stitch.
Rows 5–8: SS.
Shape top as for back.

Front:
Using cream, cast on 25 sts.
Rows 1–4: moss stitch.
Rows 5–8: SS.
Now place the heart motif, working from
the chart.

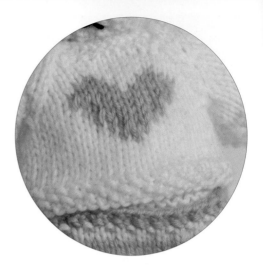

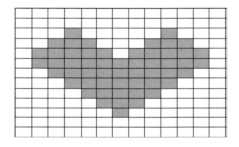

Row 9: K12, join in pink and K1, change back to
cream and K12.
Rows 10–17: continue to follow chart, and
shape armholes as for back.
When 15 sts rem, divide for neck:
Row 18: K1, skpo, K2, turn and leave rem sts on
a stitch holder.
Row 19: purl.
Row 20: K1, skpo, K1.
Row 21: purl.
Row 22: K3tog.
Fasten off.
Slip first 5 sts on to safety pin for centre neck,
join yarn to remaining sts and complete to
match back, reversing the shaping and working
K2tog in place of skpo.

Neckband:
Using cream, work in moss stitch. Pick up and knit sts across top of one sleeve, 5 sts on left side of front, 5 sts across centre neck, 5 sts on right side of front, sts from other sleeve, and finally sts from back.
Moss stitch for 3 rows.
Cast off.

Making up
Sew up the trousers, matching the stripes. Sew up the sweater and slip it over the bear's head before joining the final raglan seam and neckband. Complete the sewing up. Make a small pink bow and stitch it on to the bear's head.

Emily Knitting Bear

Materials:

1 ball pale green double knitting

1 ball white double knitting

Oddments of green, pink and yellow yarn

2 tiny pearl, heart-shaped buttons

Cocktail stick

2 small cotton balls for slippers

Fuse wire for glasses

2 small white beads for ends of knitting needles

All-purpose glue

Materials for basic bear, including light brown double knitting

Needles:

1 pair 3.25mm (UK 10; US 3) knitting needles

Instructions:

Make the basic bear (see page 6).

Dress

Back and front (both worked the same):
Using pale green, cast on 24 sts.
Rows 1–4: SS.
Rows 5–6: cast off 2 sts at beg of each row [20 sts].

Rows 7–8: SS.
Row 9: K2tog, knit to last 2 sts, K2tog.
Row 10: purl.
Rows 11–16: SS.
Rows 17–18: change to white and GS.
Cast off.
Using pale green, work skirt as for basic dress. When work measures 7cm (2¾in) change to white and work 2 rows GS.
Cast off.

Apron

Using cream, cast on 36 sts.
Rows 1–4: GS.
Row 5: knit.
Row 6: K3, purl to last 3 sts, K3.
Rows 7–16: repeat rows 5 and 6, 5 times.
Row 17: (K3, K2tog) to last 3 sts, K3 [21 sts].
Row 18: cast on 18 sts, knit to end.
Row 19: cast on 18 sts, knit to end.
Row 20: knit across all sts.
Cast off.
Work in all the yarn ends. Embroider a small flower and leaf on to one corner of the apron using pink and green.

Slippers

Using pale green, cast on 14 sts.
Row 1: knit.
Row 2: inc in each st to end [28 sts].
Continue in GS.
Rows 3–4: knit using green.
Rows 5–6: knit using pink.
Row 7: knit using green.
Complete the slippers following instructions for basic shoes on page 7, from first dec row.

Glasses

Take a short length of fuse wire and twist it around a pencil to give two small circles. Arrange them into a pleasing shape, making sure they fit over the bear's eyes. Use the photograph for guidance. Bend each end of the wire to form the arms and push them into the bear's head on each side of the eyes. Secure with a few stitches.

Knitting

Cast on 10 sts and work 18 rows GS. Do not cast off.

Making up

Lightly stuff the slippers and sew them to the bear's legs (see page 7). Sew a cotton ball to the front of each slipper. Sew the side seams on the dress, slip it on to the bear and sew the shoulder seams. Sew the two heart buttons on the front. Tie the apron around the bear's waist and secure the ties with a few stitches. Make knitting needles by breaking a cocktail stick in half and gluing a bead on to the broken end of each one. Slip the knitting on to both tiny needles, and secure the needles on to the bear's paws with a dab of glue.

Sophie Bikini Bear

Materials:

1 ball pink double knitting

Oddments of pale pink, green, blue yarn

25cm (9¾in) lilac rickrack braid

Sunglasses embellishment

Flower and leaf button

Tiny gold bead

Materials for basic bear, including dark brown
   double knitting

Needles:

1 pair 3.25mm (UK 10; US 3) knitting needles

Instructions:

Make the basic bear (see page 6).

Bikini

Top:

Using pink, cast on 40 sts.

Rows 1–4: GS.

Rows 5–6: cast off 12 sts, knit to end [16 sts].

Row 7: K8, turn and continue on this set of sts.

Rows 8–10: K2tog at end of each row [2 sts].

Row 11: K2tog [1 st].

Row 12: K1, turn.

Repeat row 12 until work measures 10cm (4in).

Fasten off.

Rejoin yarn to rem 8 sts and complete to match
the first side.

Pants:

Using pink, cast on 24 sts.

Rows 1–4: GS.

Rows 5–6: cast off 4 sts at beg of each row.

Rows 7–8: cast off 3 sts at beg of each row.

Row 9: knit.

Row 10: K2tog at each end of row [8 sts].

Rows 11–12: repeat rows 9–10 [6 sts].

Rows 13–20: GS.

Rows 21–23: inc 1 st at each end of rows 21 and
23 [10 sts].

Row 24: knit.

Rows 25–26: cast on 3 sts at beg of each row.

Rows 27–28: cast on 4 sts at beg of each row
[24 sts].

Rows 29–32: GS.

Cast off.

Beach bag

Using pale pink, cast on 12 sts.

Rows 1–2: GS.

Change to SS and work *2 rows blue, 2 rows
green, 2 rows pink*.

Repeat from * to * until a total of 13 stripes
have been worked, ending on a blue stripe.

Using pink, work 2 rows in GS.

Cast off.

Handle:

Cast on 24 sts using pale pink yarn.

Cast off.

Making up

Stitch the side seams of the bikini pants. Stitch
rickrack braid around the waist. Slip the pants
on to the bear and catch them in place with
a few stitches. Stitch braid along the bottom
edge of the bikini top. Place the top on the
bear and stitch it in place. Tie it around
the back of the neck to secure, using the
photograph as a guide. Stitch the side seams
of the bag, sew on the handle and attach the
flower and leaf button. Stitch the sunglasses to
the paw. Sew the tiny gold bead on to the front
of the bear for a belly button stud.

Poppy Panda Bear

Materials:

Oddments of black double knitting for eye patches and ears

25cm (9¾in) narrow red satin ribbon

Materials for basic bear, including black and white double knitting

Needles:

1 pair 3.25mm (UK 10; US 3) knitting needles

Instructions:

Make the basic bear (see page 6), but do not attach the eyes. Knit the head using white yarn, and the arms using black. When working the body, begin with black yarn, continue until all shaping is complete, then change to white yarn. Continue with white until you divide for the legs, then change to black yarn. Complete the legs using black. Make both sides to match.

Eye patches (make two)

Using black yarn, cast on 3 sts.
Row 1: knit.
Row 2: inc 1 st at each end of row.
Rows 3–6: GS.
Row 7: dec 1 st at each end of row.
Row 8: knit.
Row 9: sl1, k2tog, psso.
Fasten off.

Ears (make two)

Using black yarn, cast on 3 sts.
Row 1: knit.
Row 2: inc 1 st at each end of row.
Rows 3–8: GS.
Row 9: dec 1 st at each end of row.
Row 10: knit.
Row 11: sl1, k2tog, psso.
Fasten off.

Making up

Position the eye patches either side of the bear's nose, using the photograph as a guide, and stitch them in place. Sew the eyes on top of the patches. Fold the ears in half, and place them over the ears that form part of the bear's head. Gather them slightly into shape and secure. Tie a piece of red ribbon around the bear's neck.

Hector Hiking Bear

Materials:

1 ball denim blue double knitting

1 ball cream double knitting

Oddments of red, black and royal blue double knitting for backpack and boots

Small amount of safety stuffing

Materials for basic bear, including beige and light blue double knitting

Needles:

1 pair 3.25mm (UK 10; US 3) knitting needles

Instructions:

Make the basic bear (see page 6). Knit the last few rows at the bottom of each leg using light blue yarn for socks.

Special abbreviation

tw2: to twist 2 sts, miss the first st and knit into front of second st, but do not slip the second st off the needle. Knit the missed st and slip both sts off the needle together.

Sweater

Back:
Using cream, cast on 24 sts.
Rows 1–4: K2, P2 rib.
Row 5: K9, P2, tw2, P2, K9.
Row 6: P9, K2, P2, K2, P9.

Rows 7–12: continue in pattern (rows 5 and 6).
To shape armholes, continue in pattern:
Rows 13–14: cast off 2 sts at each end of row.
Row 15: K1, skpo, pattern to last 3 sts, K2tog, K1.
Row 16: purl.
Repeat rows 15 and 16 until 8 sts rem, ending with a purl row. Leave the sts on a stitch holder.

Sleeves (make two):
Using cream, cast on 24 sts.
Rows 1–4: K2, P2 rib.
Rows 5–8: SS.
Shape the top as for back, row 13 to end.

Front:
Work as for back until 14 sts rem after start of armhole shaping.
Divide for neck.
K1, skpo, K2, turn and leave rem sts on a stitch holder.
Next row: purl.
Next row: K1, skpo, K1.
Next row: purl.
Next row: sl1, K2tog, psso.
Fasten off.
Slip centre 4 sts on to a holder and work on rem 5 sts for other side. Complete to match, reversing shapings and working K2tog in place of skpo.

Neckband:
With RS facing, pick up and knit 8 sts across top of sleeve, 5 sts along left side of neck, 4 sts across neck front, 5 sts along right side of neck, 8 sts across top of second sleeve and 8 sts across neck back.
Work 5 rows SS, beg with a purl row.
Cast off loosely.

Trousers

Follow instructions for basic trousers (page 7) using denim blue.

Boots

Using black yarn, follow instructions for basic shoes on page 7. Once attached to the bear's legs, sew a few stitches using red yarn to represent laces.

Backpack

Using royal blue, cast on 14 sts.
Row 1: knit.
Row 2: K2, purl to last 2 sts, K2.
Repeat rows 1 and 2 until work measures
12cm (4¾in).
Knit 2 rows GS, cast off.

Straps:
Using black, cast on 3 sts.
Work in moss stitch for 18cm (7in).
Cast off.

Making up

Stitch the raglan seams of the sweater, leaving
the back left seam open. Stitch the side and
sleeve seams. Put the sweater on to the bear
and stitch the final seam and neckband. Sew
up the trousers and put them on to the bear.
Fold the backpack into thirds, and join the
side seams leaving the top third open for the
flap. Stuff the backpack lightly, fold over the
flap, and secure with two French knots. Sew
the centre of the strap to the middle of the
backpack at the back; catch the ends to each
side at the base of the backpack to form loops.

41

Lucky Ladybird Bear

Materials:

1 ball red double knitting

Oddments of black yarn for spots
and antennae

3 ladybird buttons

50cm (19¾in) narrow red satin ribbon

Materials for basic bear, including black and
white double knitting

Needles:

1 pair 3.25mm (UK 10; US 3) knitting needles

Instructions:

Make the basic bear (see page 6) using black
for the body, legs and arms and cream for
the head.

Wings (make two)

Work all inc sts for the wings by picking up the
strand of yarn between the previous 2 sts and
knitting into the back of it.
Using red, cast on 5 sts.
Row 1: purl.
Row 2: K2, inc, K1, inc, K2 [7 sts].
Row 3: knit.
Row 4: K3, inc, K1, inc, K3 [9 sts].
Row 5: knit.
Row 6: K4, inc, K1, inc, K4 [11 sts].
Row 7: knit.
Row 8: K5, inc, K1, inc, K5 [13 sts].
Continue to inc in this manner
until 25 sts are on the needle
Work 8 rows GS.
Dec 1 st at each end of each alt
row until 7 sts rem.
Cast off.

Spots (make 6):
Using black, cast on 3 sts. Work in GS.
Row 1: knit.
Row 2: inc 1 st at each end of row.
Rows 3–6: GS.
Row 7: dec 1 st at each end of row.
Row 8: knit.
Row 9: sl1, K2tog, psso.
Fasten off.

Making up

Stitch three spots on each wing. Attach the
wings to the bear, overlapping them slightly
at the back neck. Tie the ribbon around the
ladybird bear's neck. Make the antennae by
threading a piece of black yarn through the
top of the head and roll each end into a tight
circle. Secure them with a few stitches. Sew the
buttons on to the front of the bear.

Pretty Party Bear

Materials:

1 ball cream double knitting

1 ball turquoise double knitting

6 heart-shaped turquoise glass beads

50cm (19¾in) narrow, fine ribbon with turquoise edging

Small amount of safety stuffing

Materials for basic bear, including brown double knitting

Needles:

1 pair 3.25mm (UK 10; US 3) knitting needles

Instructions:

Make the basic bear (see page 6), working the last 5 rows of each leg in turquoise to represent socks.

Dress

Work two pieces the same, front and back (working from neck edge):
Using cream, cast on 18 sts.
Rows 1–8: K1, P1 rib.
Row 9: (K1, inc in next st) to end of row [27 sts].
Row 10: purl.
Row 11: K2, (yfwd, K2tog, K1) to last st, K1.
Row 12: purl.
Rows 13–14: SS, ending with a purl row.

Row 15: join in turquoise. K1 cream, K1 turquoise, (K3 cream, K1 turquoise) across row to last st, K1 cream. Break turquoise yarn.
Row 16: purl.
Row 17: inc 1 st at each end of row [29 sts].
Row 18: purl.
Rows 19–20: SS.
Row 21: inc 1 st at each end of row [31 sts].
Row 22: purl.
Row 23–25: repeat rows 15–17 [33 sts].
Rows 26–30: SS, ending with a purl row.
Rows 31–32: Join in turquoise and knit 2 rows.
Cast off in GS.

Shoulder straps (make two):
Using cream, cast on 3 sts.
Row 1: K1, P1, K1.
Repeat row 1 until work measures 4cm (1½in).
Cast off.

Handbag

Using cream, cast on 10 sts.
Row 1: K2, P6, K2.
Row 2: (RS facing) knit.
Repeat rows 1 and 2 until work measures 4cm (1½in).

To shape flap of bag:
Row 1: K2, skpo, K2, K2tog, K2.
Row 2: K2, P4, K2.
Row 3: K2, skpo, K2tog, K2.
Row 4: K2, P2, K2.
Row 5: K2, K2tog, K2.
Row 6: K2, P1, K2.
Row 7: K1, sl1, K2tog, psso, K1.
Row 8: K3.
Row 9: K3tog.
Fasten off.

Handle:
Using turquoise, cast on 2 sts.
Row 1: K1, P1.
Row 2: P1, K1.
Repeat rows 1 and 2 until work measures 4cm (1½in).
Cast off.

Shoes

Using cream yarn, follow instructions for basic shoes on page 7. When you have attached them to the bear, sew a heart button on the front of each one.

Making up

Sew the side seams of the dress up to the start of the ribbing. Match the patterns and the GS hem. Stitch one end of each shoulder strap on to the top of the dress. Slip the dress on to the bear. Pass the straps over the bear's shoulders and stitch them to the other side of the dress. Secure, and stitch a heart bead on to the ends of the straps at the front. Thread ribbon through the holes at the waist and tie in a bow. Make another tiny bow and sew it to the bear's head. Fold the piece of knitting for the handbag into thirds to make an envelope shape. Stitch the side seams. Attach a heart bead to the point of the flap. Thread the handle under the flap and secure.

Ellie Bouquet Bear

Materials:

1 ball pale blue double knitting

Oddment of deep turquoise and green yarn

50cm (19¾in) deep turquoise narrow velvet ribbon

2 small sparkly, flower-shaped buttons

Tiny bunch of paper or silk flowers

Materials for basic bear, including pale beige double knitting

Needles:

1 pair 3.25mm (UK 10; US 3) knitting needles

Instructions:

Make the basic bear (see page 6).

Dress
Using pale blue yarn, follow instructions for basic dress (see page 7).
When skirt measures 4cm (1½in), change to deep turquoise and work a further 4 rows SS, followed by 3 rows GS.
Cast off.

Sleeve frills (make two):
Using pale blue, cast on 24 sts loosely.
Row 1: purl.
Row 2: knit, inc 12 sts evenly across row [36 sts].
Rows 3–4: SS.
Row 5: change to deep turquoise and knit 1 row.
Cast off.

Shoes
Using turquoise yarn, follow instructions for basic shoes on page 7. When you have attached them to the bear, sew a sparkly button on the front of each one.

Making up

Stitch one shoulder seam and work the neckband in deep turquoise. Sew the side seams, and turn right-side out. Slip the dress on to the bear. Catch together the neckband and shoulder seam neatly. Sew the sleeve frill ends together then stitch them to the armholes, easing to fit if needed. Tie a length of ribbon around the waist and finish with a bow at the back of the dress. Wrap some green yarn tightly around the base of the flowers, and secure. Catch the bear's paws to each side of the flowers to hold them in place. Tie a small bow from some ribbon and sew it to the top of the bear's head.

Acknowledgements

Many thanks to Coats Patons for their kind donation of many of the yarns used to make my bears. Thank you also to my family and friends who have helped and inspired me whilst working on my book.

Publishers' Note

If you would like more information on knitting techniques, try the *Beginner's Guide to Knitting* by Alison Dupernex, Search Press, 2004; the *Compendium of Knitting Techniques* by Betty Barnden*, Search Press, 2008; *Start to Knit* by Alison Dupernex, Search Press, 2008; and *The Knitting Stitch Bible* by Maria Parry Jones*, Search Press, 2009.

* Not published by Search Press in the USA.